Kissing Toads

Cath Tate

VIRAGO

Before you meet your handsome prince, you have to kiss a lot of toads.

Cath Tate was born in London in 1951. She spent three years at York University and then taught for nine years in a south London comprehensive. Since the arrival of the Thatcher government she has been producing political photomontages. These have appeared in innumerable publications and are widely distributed as postcards and posters. She now lives and works in London.

With thanks to Dave Bradshaw, Kath Burlinson,
John Chapman, Sheila Gray, Pam Isherwood,
Peter Kennard, Mhairi Macleod, Jenny Matthews,
Lorraine Pascoe, Sue Preece, Brenda Prince, Rose Spilberg,
Les Tate, Rosemary Tate and Lesley Whitfield.

Published by Virago Press 1987
41 William IV Street, London WC2N 4DB

Copyright © Cath Tate 1987

British Library Cataloguing in Publication Data

Tate, Cath
Kissing toads.
1. Tate, Cath
I. Title
779'.092'4 TR685

ISBN 0-86068-926-3

Printed in Great Britain

Vote for me because I am smooth and well-heeled and I employ an expensive advertising agency and I like my picture on the telly and in the papers that are owned by some great friends of mine.

Political Portraits

A Special Relationship

A Minister of Defence

In Charge of the Piggy Bank

Norman Tebbit demonstrates the
Tory answer to unemployment

Norman

David Owen: the doggie with the policies that won't make a
mess on your carpet

Michael Foot: Adrift June 1983

Watering down the policies

Making a Killing

(being an explanation of the Free World and the market
forces that promote individual excellence)

Running for Britain

Bread not Bombs

Hello, I'm a teddy made
north of the Watford Gap

Hi, I'm a pink mouse made
in Taiwan. The Free Market
says that if someone makes
me there they don't have to
be paid a living wage

The Free Market says that I can smash teddy right out of the
market place because I am cheaper than him

Hi, I'm a user friendly gun. I'm now more profitable to make than toys since everyone in the west is unemployed and can't afford to buy them and everyone in the east earns so little they can't afford them either

What is the point of making things if only *poor* people want them? *Rich* people want to buy me so they can go and shoot Russians who refuse to buy pink mice and teddies

You must *try* to understand that I only shoot people for *your* good and to defend the FREE WORLD

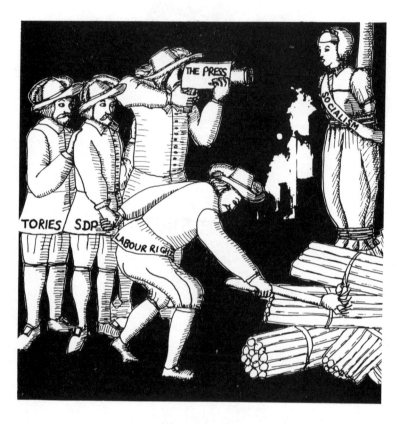

Burning Witches

The Big Bang: the Stock Exchange takes off

I'm all right Jack, I live in Esher

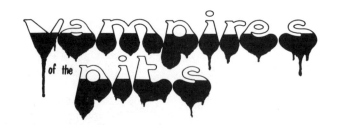

This Christmas give your child a radioactive cuddle

The Arts under
Private Sponsorship
present

FAG END CIGARETTES

production of

THE MARCH OF THE PHILISTINES

A Tory cultural evening

"Art sponsorship at its most outstanding."

Warning from HM Government: The Safety Curtain will remain down throughout the performance to ensure that no subversive ideas escape to the audience.

The Evening's Viewing

A Monstrous
Regiment of Men

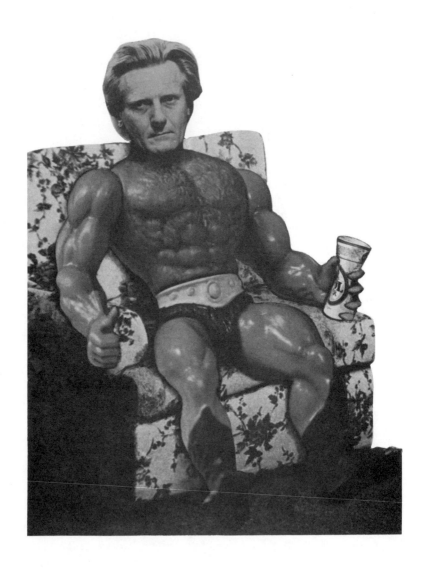

Star Wars

The Men at the Dinner Party

There, there dear

Law and Order

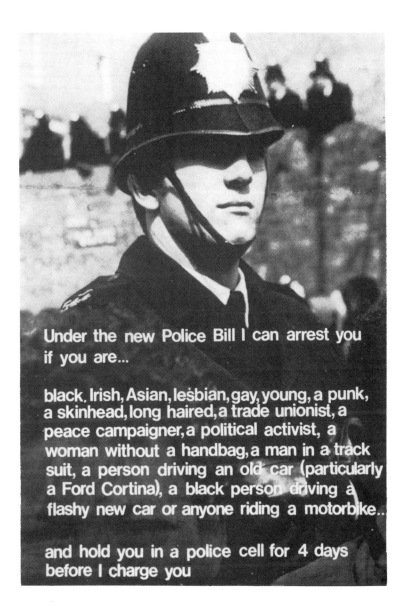

Under the new Police Bill I can arrest you if you are...

black, Irish, Asian, lesbian, gay, young, a punk, a skinhead, long haired, a trade unionist, a peace campaigner, a political activist, a woman without a handbag, a man in a track suit, a person driving an old car (particularly a Ford Cortina), a black person driving a flashy new car or anyone riding a motorbike...

and hold you in a police cell for 4 days before I charge you

Construction in
burnt steel
Sculpture generously
donated by
Mrs Thatcher to the
people of Brixton
with the aid of the
Metropolitan Police

Have you ever seen a judge on a bus?

(In 1981 the Law Lords declared that the GLC's cheap fares policy was illegal)

Moles Unearth Worms

The Thatcher Years

Stuff You All

The Hooligan

Postcard 1983

South London Hospital 1987

Let them eat bricks

"I've never found it difficult to understand peoples' problems. I have experienced so many of them myself."
Mrs Thatcher 1975

'Out damned spot! out I say! ... What need we fear who knows it, when none can call our power to account? Yet who would have thought the old man to have had so much blood in him?'

— Lady Macbeth

Christmas card 1981

The Ghost of Christmas present

Cuts in Health
Unemployment
Poor Housing
Cruise Missiles
Poverty

Christmas card 1983

Prevent Street Crime

Newspaper
Between the Ears

Shipwrecked Democracy

THE MALE

VIRUS SCARE HITS TORIES

GAY YOUTH MUGS FLEET ST EDITOR

TURN TO PAGE 5

MRS THATCHER was today the latest victim of the recently discovered rabies virus that attacks members of the Tory party.

The disease gives the sufferers the delusion that the unemployment figures are coming down and that prosperity is returning to Britain. The Tories are particularly vulnerable to this virus since very few of them have any contact with those areas of the country most affected by their policies.

PLUS
PAGE 3
EXCLUSIVE

The secrets of Norman Tebbit

I saw the lot, says his butler

DI BEATS THE BOMB!

It's quickly back to normal for Princess Di seen here visiting Croydon shopping centre after the recent nuke attack on Potters Bar. Fresh and stunning as usual the Princess sparkled in one of her famous hats made for her by her favourite young designer. With this visit Di has certainly shown us what duty means. You show us Di!

Check Mate!

★ 30-year-old Terry is not just a handsome face, he is also a champion chess player. You would never get bored with him around. I bet he knows where to put his pieces!

Family Life

Our Suburban Dream

The Joys of Family Life No 1:
Travelling on buses with small children and large shopping bags

The Joys of Family Life No 2:
Feeding the Family

The Upholder of Family Life:
The politician that stalks the shopping centre during elections

Behind every great man

Behind every great woman

Holding up Half the Sky

Biting Beauty

The Dish of the Day

Dinner on the Grass

Photograph

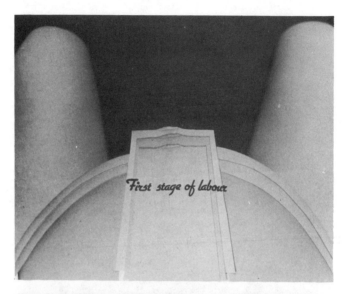

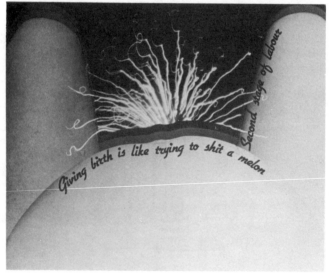

Childbirth I and II

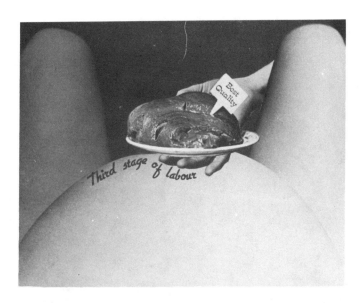

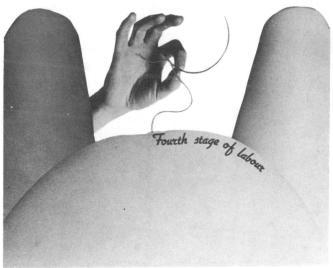

Childbirth III and IV

The Great Escape

Epilogue